PUPPET FUN

PUPPET FUN

Production, Performance and Plays

Nellie McCaslin

Illustrated with photographs by
Helen King
and with drawings by
Daty Healy

DAVID McKAY COMPANY, INC.
New York

Library of Congress Cataloging in Publication Data

McCaslin, Nellie.
Puppet fun.

SUMMARY: Describes the construction of puppets and
small theater stages. Also includes several plays with
staging instructions.
1. Puppets and puppets-plays—Juvenile literature.
[1. Puppets and puppet-plays] I. Title.
PN1972.M16 791.5′3 77-2438
ISBN 0-679-20416-4

10 9 8 7 6 5 4 3 2 1

MANUFACTURED IN THE UNITED STATES OF AMERICA

To my niece, Alexandra Plotkin,
who delights in books of all kinds.

Contents

PUPPET FUN

Introduction

People all over the world love puppets. In our country they are most popular with children. This book shows you how to make some of the simpler kinds of puppets. It also tells some of the things you can do with them. If you like to act, you'll find a world of ideas for you and your puppets to perform.

Most of the puppets you make will be small. They can act in small places, such as the top of a table or a box. You don't need a stage, but later on, you may want to make one.

Puppets aren't dolls, although they often resemble them. Puppets are "actors," who come to life with the help of a puppeteer.

Almost any object can be a puppet: a toy, a tool, a hairbrush, a lollipop, a spoon, a broom. Even your hand can be a puppet if you move it and speak so that your hand seems to be doing the walking and talking.

Introduction

CHAPTER ONE
Almost Anything Can Be a Puppet

Just to prove it, try out a few things. Kneel behind a table and move an object along the edge of it. Keep your hand out of sight so that the object seems to be doing the moving. Here are a few things you can use.

A wooden spoon. Make it walk, run, jump, disappear.

A toy. A teddy bear or a rag doll will do. They

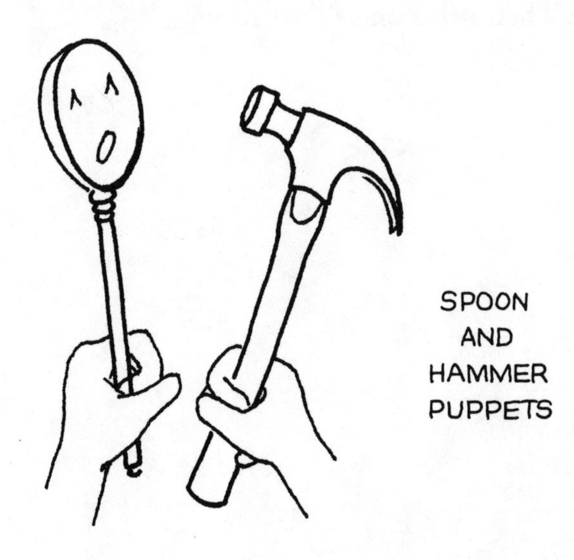

SPOON AND HAMMER PUPPETS

are soft and move in different ways from the spoon. Sometimes toys make fine puppets, but it's not a good idea to depend on them. The puppets you make yourself will almost always be better.

A pencil. A ruler. A lollipop. An artificial flower. They'll all become different characters when you start moving them. Now try holding one in each hand. What happens when a pencil and a ruler meet?

Your own hands. What can they do that the other things couldn't do? Hands make wonderful movements. Let them walk, dance, jump, fight, bow, march off.

Look around for some other objects that haven't been mentioned. Invent actions for them, and decide what kinds of characters they seem to be. Remember that *you* make the puppet. It's not alive till you move it. Then it becomes part of you.

CHAPTER TWO
How to Make Puppets

There are many different kinds of puppets. Some hang from strings; some are fastened to sticks called rods. Others slip on the hand like gloves. Some puppets are as tall as a person and must be pushed. In this book we're going to concentrate on only one kind—the hand puppet and its many variations. They include the bandana puppet, the finger puppet, the paper bag puppet, the flat puppet, the sock puppet, and the glove puppet.

BANDANA PUPPETS

The easiest one to begin with is the bandana puppet. Put a bandana or cloth over your hand. Let your first and middle fingers be the "head," and put a rubber band around them for the neck. Your thumb and little finger are the arms. Put rubber bands around them in order to hold the cloth in place. Imagine that your hand is the actor. Make your "puppet" clap its hands, shake its head, and fall down.

You can do many more things with a bandana

puppet. For instance, try cutting a hole in the middle of the bandana, and poking your first and second fingers through it. Now take a styrofoam ball with a hole scooped out for your fingers. Heads can be made out of different things: a small paper cup, an apple (after you have cut out the core), or a ball.

FINGER PUPPETS

Finger puppets are the smallest of all puppets. They slip on the fingers, and you can play with them or use them with larger hand puppets to show different sized characters. For instance, a finger puppet might be an elf and a hand puppet a man.

One way to make finger puppets is to sew them of felt. First, make a pattern. Put your hand down flat on a piece of paper, and draw around your fingers with a pencil. Be sure to add a little extra material all the way around to allow for the sewing.

Next, cut out the paper patterns and pin them on a piece of felt. You'll have to cut two shapes for each puppet. Put the two shapes together and sew around the edges. Leave the bottom open for your finger.

Another easy way to make finger puppets is to cut the fingers off an old glove. White gloves are the best because you can put faces on them. Slip the glove fingers over your own and—presto—you'll have five little puppets! You can cut circles and paint faces on them. When the paint is dry, they can be pasted on the puppets.

PAPER BAG PUPPETS

The paper bag puppet is one of the best to begin with because bags come in all sizes and are easily obtainable. Also, if you happen to tear your bag, chances are there's another one just like it in your home. You can make adult and children puppets or giants and elves with different sizes of bags.

Small bags will fit on your hands, while big bags can go over your head. If you wear a bag on your head you'll need to cut holes in it for your eyes and mouth. Next, paint a face on the bag. You can use your hands, your head, or even your feet for puppets. Hands work best, though, because you can do so many more things with them.

You can paint and paste on paper bags and, if the paper is thick enough, you can even sew on them. A bag can be just a head or a whole puppet.

FLAT PUPPETS

Flat puppets are really rod puppets, but they're included here because they're easy to make and can be used with other kinds of puppets. Flat puppets are a little like paper dolls. You can cut them out of cardboard and paste them on tongue depressors or tie them on sticks. Hold the puppet attached to a stick

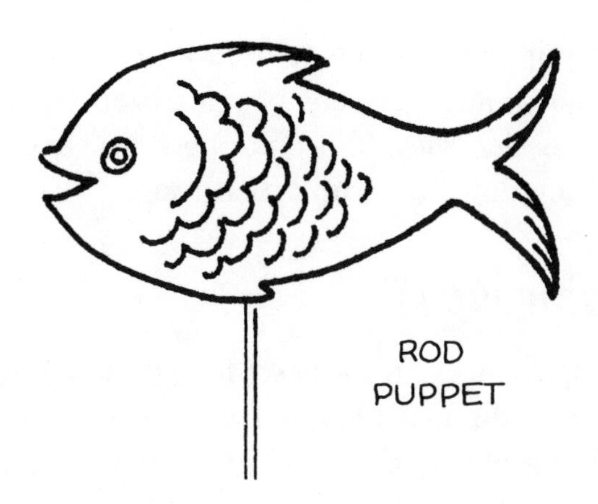

in your hand, just below the edge of the table. When you move it, the puppet will seem to be walking along by itself.

Flat puppets may be colored and dressed. Animals make good flat puppets because you have only to draw the side view. Flat puppets are easy to keep, since they don't take up much room.

SHADOW PUPPETS

Flat puppets can be used for shadow shows, also. To give a shadow play, all you need are some flat puppets, a sheet, and a lamp. When you move the

puppets behind the sheet, they cast shadows on it. The closer they are to the sheet, the stronger the shadow, or silhouette, will be.

SOCK PUPPETS

A sock makes a very good puppet because it stretches yet won't slip off your hand. You can do many things with a sock puppet, such as making it into a mouth. Take an old sock and put your hand inside it. Put your fingers into the toe, and put your thumb into the heel. You now have the upper and

lower jaws of a mouth. Bring them together in a big bite! If you add eyes and other markings, you can create a bird, a wolf, a crocodile, or a dragon. You can make your puppet mouth more exciting by sewing a piece of red felt inside it and adding a tongue.

GLOVE PUPPETS

The glove puppet needs more sewing than the others. It has to be cut out of cloth and then sewn together. It may also have a separate head.

First, take a piece of strong cotton cloth and double it. Felt is good, if you have it, because it won't ravel. Other materials will do, however, so use what you have on hand.

> Cut a pattern of newspaper for your puppet. There should be a head and two arms, and the pattern must be large enough to fit your hand.
>
> Pin the pattern to the material and trace around it.
>
> Remove the pattern and cut out the puppet.
>
> Keep the two pieces of cloth together and sew around the edges, remembering to leave the bottom open for your hand to go through.
>
> A felt puppet is ready to use as it is. A puppet made of a softer material should be turned inside out to keep it from raveling.

You'll probably want to put a face on your puppet. Eyes, nose, and mouth can be drawn or embroidered on it. Buttons make excellent eyes and yarn makes good hair. A little stuffing makes the head rounder.

If you want to make a separate head, a lightweight material such as papier mâché or styrofoam, for instance, will work well. It's a good idea to decorate

GLOVE
PUPPETS

the head first. Then slip it over your second and third fingers. Although it's harder to handle a puppet with a separate head than a puppet that's in one piece, you'll soon learn how to manage it if you practice.

GIANT PUPPETS

Some puppeteers have puppets as tall as they are. These giant puppets are made of lightweight material so they can be pushed or carried. Sometimes the puppeteers even get inside them. Unless you have a yard or a playroom, however, you probably won't be making life-size puppets. For those of you who want to try, here are some ways to make them.

The easiest way to make a giant puppet is to put a paper bag or papier mâché head on a broomstick or pole. Then hang a blanket or cape on it and hide inside the covering. You can then carry the stick, while you are hidden under the blanket.

Another way to make a giant puppet is to use a tall, narrow cardboard box. Your supermarket has nice, clean ones. Paint a face and clothes on the box. Even a big box can be moved easily.

Figures made of newspaper and paste are harder to make, and they take a long time to dry. If you have a good place to work, these papier mâché figures are fun to make. They should be hollow so you can get inside them, or flat so you can push them from behind.

MATERIALS

In order to put on a puppet show, you'll need several kinds of materials. You probably won't have to buy anything in a store because you may be able

to find everything you need in your own home. Scraps of paper, cloth, boxes of all sizes, sticks, styrofoam, and even lollipops will come in handy.

Here's a list of materials you might start with:

- paper bags of all sizes
- string, paste, scissors, crayons, magic markers, safety pins
- scraps of cloth
- bandanas and old scarfs
- styrofoam balls (always available at Christmas, but many people save them from year to year)
- small paper cups
- old socks
- tablet backs
- small sticks, tongue depressors
- ribbons, yarn, buttons, needles, and thread
- a big carton in which to keep your materials

CHAPTER THREE
Making Your Puppets Perform

Now that you've made some puppets, your next step is to make them perform. You may have tried out different objects to see how they worked, but there's more to it than that. Like human actors, puppets have to show feelings, move, and speak so they can be heard and understood.

HOLDING YOUR PUPPET

There are different ways of holding puppets. There's no one right way. Just use the way that

works best for you. Try putting different fingers in positions for the arms and head. When you find the position that's most comfortable for you, use it. Many puppeteers put their second and third fingers in the neck, their fourth and fifth fingers in one arm, and their thumb in the other. Some people have longer fingers than others, so this method doesn't suit everyone.

Puppets can be held either in front of you or over your head. Again, use whichever way that's easier for you. If you're playing for a long time, it's usually more comfortable to work the puppet in front of your face.

If you decide to hold your puppet that way, you'll be seen by the audience. This doesn't matter. The audience, when you have one, will soon forget you're there. If you want to hang a curtain between you and your puppets, you'll need a stage. A dark, lightweight piece of cloth at the back of the stage will hide you and make your puppets stand out. If the cloth is semi-transparent, you can see through it without being seen.

SOME BASIC ACTIONS

Moving the puppet's head up and down means "yes." Shaking it from side to side means "no."

When the puppet's hands point to itself, it means "me" or "mine." Moving one of its hands toward its body means "come here." Waving its hand may mean either "hello" or "goodbye."

Clapping its hands together may mean it is happy or excited. Touching the head with a hand means thinking. Bobbing the head suddenly while you sneeze backstage makes the puppet seem to be doing the sneezing.

Walking, running, and jumping can be suggested by the way you move the puppet across the stage. Try not to lift it up in the air. You'll soon get the knack of holding it down, so that it seems to be doing all the moving.

TWO PUPPETS

When you and a friend are puppeteering together, the chances are you'll each be holding a puppet. This

is harder than playing alone, but it's more fun. You'll each have to watch out that your puppets don't bump into each other. Also, when one puppet is speaking, the other one should remember to listen.

Occasionally there will be a scene for three puppets. This takes some doing for three people will have to work together backstage, or one person will have to handle two puppets. It's a good idea, at first, to use stories that have no more than two characters on the stage at one time.

EXPRESSING FEELINGS

Your puppet must show feelings, as well as move and talk. Try to find ways of showing that your puppet feels:

angry
excited
shy
tired
happy
curious
scared
hungry

Now see if you can put the proper action with a feeling. For example, show that your puppet is:

curious–and looks into a box
angry–and hits someone
happy–and claps its hands for joy
thinking–and comes up with an idea

SPEAKING

When you are in a play, you try to speak loudly enough to be heard and clearly enough to be understood. The same thing holds true for puppeteers, except that they must be even clearer. If you are playing two parts, which may often be the case, then you must use two different voices. You'll find this easy when you begin to feel the difference between the characters.

Just for fun, have your puppet talk like

your mother
your father
your grandmother
an angry neighbor
your best friend
your teacher

Now make it talk like

a giant
an elf
Little Red Riding Hood
the Wolf
Cinderella
her Fairy Godmother

Soon you'll be able to speak in lots of different voices. Remember, your puppets are the actors, but they depend on you to make them act.

A puppet should move when it speaks, just enough to let the audience know who is talking. This also helps to give life to the puppet.

HANDLING PROPS

A word about props. Props are objects, such as a basket or food, used by actors in a play. They should be large in proportion to the size of the puppet. There are two reasons for this. It makes it easier for the puppeteer to pick them up; and the audience can see the prop more easily.

CHAPTER FOUR

The Puppet Stage

In the first place, it's not necessary to have a stage. Puppets can act anywhere. All you really need is a smooth surface, about three feet long. A table, a coffee table, a bench, a desk, or a box will do. Or you can stretch a blanket across a doorway and let your puppets perform above it.

If you don't want to be seen while you're working, you can put a little screen on the table in front of you. The screen should measure from one to one-and-a-half feet high (or about one-half meter), and extend across the area you are using for your stage. If you

use a screen, be sure it's heavy enough to stand up by itself. If it's cardboard, it should be taped to the table so that it won't fall down in the middle of your show.

Another idea for a stage is a cardboard box with the front and back cut off. Hang a thin piece of material across the back of the box; your puppets will act in front of it. All this takes more work, as well as a place to put your stage when not in use. But a stage adds a professional touch. A lamp placed in front of the box will help to light it.

CHAPTER FIVE

Stories for Puppet Plays

Your puppets should act without scripts because you'll have your hands full just moving the puppets. If you know the story you're presenting, you can make up the words as you go along. Besides, it will sound more natural.

There are two things to remember about stories for puppet plays. First, use stories that have no more than two or three puppets on the stage at one time. This doesn't mean there can't be more characters in the story. It just means that they should not all be on the stage at once.

Second, know the story so well that you won't forget any part of it. If you like it, chances are you know it by heart anyhow. A variety of stories that make good puppet plays are included in this book, and there are hundreds of others. Try your favorites.

SCENERY

You don't need scenery, but sometimes you may want it. If you do, make it out of cardboard or stiff paper. Be sure to fasten it so that it won't fall down.

Doll furniture can be used, if it's the right size. A background is usually all you need to show where the story takes place. You don't even need that if the puppets tell the audience where the play is taking place.

STONE SOUP

Stone Soup is a good story for two puppets. You can handle both of them, or you and a friend can put on the play together.

Characters

An Old Woman
A Tramp

(This is an Irish tale that tells how a clever tramp played a trick on a stingy old woman.)

The Old Woman is sitting, as usual, in her cottage kitchen, planning how she will make soup for her supper.

"I'll put in potatoes and onions, green peas, and that ham bone that was left from Sunday dinner," the Old Woman says to herself.

At that moment a Tramp appears at the door and knocks politely.

"May I stop here and rest a bit?" he asks.

The Old Woman eyes him with suspicion, but she says he can sit down on her doorstep. The Tramp sits down and begins to talk to her pleasantly. Finally he asks if she would give him a bite of supper.

The Old Woman refuses. She says that she lives alone and has very little food in the house. The Tramp nods in sympathy. Then he says he knows a way to make soup from a stone. If she will just put a pot of water on the stove, he will make enough soup for both of them.

"Stone soup?" screams the Old Woman. *"Whoever heard of that?"*

"Well," says the Tramp, *"I shall be glad to make you some. I'll bet that you find it the best soup you ever ate."*

The Old Woman agrees to get him a pot of water. Then the Tramp goes out to the yard to find the right stone. In a moment he returns. He drops the stone into the pot and begins to stir. *"May I have a pinch of salt?"* he asks. *"Salt always improves the flavor."*

The Old Woman gives him the salt. Then he asks for some pepper. He tastes the water. *"Do you have an onion? Onions are always good in soup."*

By this time, the Old Woman is enjoying herself, so she brings him an onion. *"Just right,"* he says. *"I'll take my knife and cut it up in little pieces. Like this."* Next he asks for two or three potatoes and a few carrots or peas. Finally he asks if she happens to have a ham bone in the house. *"For flavor,"* he adds.

The soup is now beginning to smell very good. The Old Woman is delighted. The two talk of the Tramp's travels until he decides that the soup is ready to eat. *"What about a slice of bread and some butter? That would go well with it."*

The Old Woman agrees, and she goes to get it.

"Now," says the Tramp, as he gives her a spoon, *"taste for yourself."*

The Old Woman takes a spoonful. *"Why,"* she exclaims, *"it's the best soup I ever ate in my life! And to think it was made from a stone!"*

LITTLE INDIAN TWO FEET'S HORSE

Characters

Little Indian Two Feet
His Horse

This story can be played just as it is, or you can make it longer by adding adventures. Since Indian Two Feet is a little boy who talks to himself, we know what is happening. You can make the horse move by bending your hand so that the arms of the puppet become its front legs. Try out some movements until you find the ones that are right. The horse may be a flat puppet instead of a glove puppet.

Little Indian Two Feet wants a horse more than anything else in the world. He often walks on the prairie, dreaming of the horse he will someday own. His father has told him that he can have a horse when he gets older. That seems far away to a boy of ten! So, one morning Little Indian Two Feet decides to go out and see if he can find a horse. Perhaps if he hunts long enough, he'll see one on the prairie, a horse that no one owns. He walks and he walks. He calls and he calls, but no horse answers. He climbs a hill, he looks over it, and he calls again. Still no horse comes to him.

He manages to cross a wide stream by a meadow. Two Feet walks in the tall grass until he is tired, but there are no horses grazing anywhere. Finally he decides to lie down and rest before he starts home.

In no time at all Two Feet falls fast asleep. While he is sleeping, a pony appears. It is a colt, one of the wild ponies that run loose on the prairie. In fact, it is so young a colt that it knows no fear. Since it has never seen a boy before it steps up to look at him. The pony puts its soft nose against Two Feet's cheek and rubs against it. Two Feet awakens with a start! He can hardly believe his eyes. He sits up and touches the pony's shoulder. *"Did you come to me?"* he asks. *"Do you want to go home with me?"*

The pony nods his head as if to say *"yes."* Little Two Feet puts his arm on the pony's neck and the two of them go off together. Little Two Feet has found his horse.

THE FISHERMAN AND HIS WIFE

Characters

The Fisherman
His Wife
The Flounder

The Fisherman and His Wife is another good story for puppets to play. You don't need any scenery. If you want to show the different houses, you can draw pictures of them and put them up behind the puppets.

A poor Fisherman lives with his wife in a cottage by the sea. Every day he goes down to the shore to catch a fish for their supper. When his luck is good, he has enough fish to sell to their neighbors. One morning the Fisherman goes out as usual and sits down in his favorite fishing spot. Suddenly there is a tug on his line. He pulls and he pulls.

"What have I caught?" asks the Fisherman. He gives another tug on his line and up comes the biggest flounder he has ever seen.

Then, to his amazement, the fish speaks. *"Please let me go. I have done you no harm."*

The Fisherman can't believe his ears. *"You can talk? I have never heard of a fish that could talk."*

"I was once a prince," says the Flounder sadly. *"An evil spell was put on me, and I am doomed to spend the rest of my life as a fish."*

"I am sorry if I've hurt you," says the Fisherman, taking the hook from the fish. *"Go back to your home in the sea."*

"Oh, thank you," the Flounder says. *"You have saved my life. If I can ever do anything for you, call on me. I'm never far away."*

The Fisherman promises the Flounder that he will do so. Then, eager to tell his wife about his strange adventure, he packs up and goes home. When he has finished his tale, his wife scolds him for his stupidity. *"That's just like you! Why didn't you ask him for a nice house and some food for our dinner? He was a magic fish and you let him go."*

"I'm sorry, wife," says the Fisherman. *"I didn't think of it."*

"Well, go back down to the sea and ask for a house like our neighbor's, with enough food to last us a year."

"Very well," replies the Fisherman. So he goes down to the place where he had caught the Flounder and calls out:

"Oh, fish of the sea,
come listen to me.
For my wife, my wife, the plague of my life,
Has sent me to ask a boon of thee."

Scarcely does he finish when the Flounder appears.

"What can I do for you?" the fish asks politely.

The Fisherman tells him.

"No sooner asked then granted," says the fish. *"Go home and you will find a house like your neighbor's."*

The Fisherman hurries home, and there is a beautiful stone house where his little cottage had been. His wife appears at the door, delighted with their good fortune.

For a time the Fisherman and his wife live happily. Then one morning his wife, who is always discontented, says, *"I don't know why you asked for this house. I should like a castle with servants to wait on me."*

"This house is plenty good enough," says her husband.

"No," she replies, *"Go back and tell the fish I must have a castle."*

The Fisherman doesn't want to do her bidding, but at last he agrees. He goes down to the sea and again calls out:

"Oh, fish of the sea,
come listen to me.
For my wife, my wife, the plague of my life,
Has sent me to ask a boon of thee."

In a flash the Flounder appears. *"Nothing easier,"* he says, after the Fisherman explains the matter to him. *"Go home to your castle."*

Then the Flounder disappears and the Fisherman returns home. Instead of the stone house, there is a great castle with towers and walls surrounding it. His wife is overjoyed. But after a time, she again becomes discontented.

She sends her husband back to the Flounder many times. She wants to be the richest woman in the world. Then a Queen. Next, an Empress. And finally, Goddess of the Universe. Each time her husband begs her to be content with what they have, but she will not listen. And each time the fish grants her wish—until the last one.

"What is it now?" the Flounder asks the Fisherman.

"Oh, gracious Flounder," replies the Fisherman, "*my wife wants to be Goddess of the Universe.*"

"Never!" declares the Flounder angrily. *"I will grant no more wishes. Your wife can return to her cottage."*

There is a loud noise like a clap of thunder and the

fish disappears. Then the Fisherman goes home, where he finds his wife in the doorway of their humble cottage.

THE BLACKSMITH AND THE CARPENTER

Characters

A Rich Man
A Blacksmith
A Carpenter

A Rich Man lives in a big house in the center of a village. Down the road on one side lives a Blacksmith. Down the road on the other side lives a Carpenter. Now, the Rich Man hates noise. All day long he hears the pounding of the Carpenter and the loud clang-clang of the Blacksmith's hammer on his anvil.

At last the Rich Man decides he can stand the noise no longer, so he sets out to make a bargain with his neighbors. First, he goes to the Carpenter and offers him a large sum of money if he will move from his house. At first the Carpenter refuses, but in time he accepts the Rich Man's offer.

Next the Rich Man goes to the Blacksmith and shouts above the noise that he will pay him well to find another shop. Finally, the Blacksmith agrees and the Rich Man goes home, pleased with his day's work.

Now the Carpenter and the Blacksmith are good friends, and they immediately tell each other of the

Rich Man's visit. But they are faced with a problem: where will they move? Suddenly the Carpenter has an idea. Why not exchange houses? The Blacksmith agrees. That night they move into each other's houses.

The Rich Man, who is enjoying the peace and quiet, smiles at his cleverness. *"There is nothing money can't buy,"* he says to himself. But the silence is suddenly shattered when the Carpenter and the Blacksmith begin their day's work!

THE POT OF GOLD

Characters

A Farmer
His Two Lazy Sons

There is a Farmer who has two Lazy Sons. Every day he asks them to work in his fields, but they always give one excuse or another for not helping him. They like good times, and they spend money freely. One day, however, they go to their father and ask him for money to pay their debts. Instead of giving in, as he always has, the Farmer tells them there is a pot of gold buried in the vineyard near by. *"It is yours, if you can find it,"* says the old man.

The two young men run out to the vineyard and begin digging up the earth. They find nothing. But in the process of looking, they cultivate the vineyard. That autumn there is a wonderful crop of grapes.

The Farmer tells his sons it is worth a pot of gold. If they will pick and sell the grapes, they can keep the money. This will pay their debts and more.

This is an old fable that makes a good play as it is. Can you use the same idea but make it into a modern story?

THE LANTERN AND THE FAN

Characters

Father-in-law
First Daughter-in-law
Second Daughter-in-law

In Japan there lives a rich man, whose sons are married to two sisters from a distant town. The rich man is very fond of his Daughters-in-law, and they are happy in their new home. But after a while, they long to see their family again. Their Father-in-law does not want them to leave because his sons are away and it will be lonely with no one about. He finally agrees, however, but only on the condition that they return in a fortnight.

"If you are not back by that time," he says, *"you must bring me gifts to show your affection."*

He turns to the older sister and says, *"You are to bring me fire wrapped in paper."* Then he turns to the younger sister and says, *"You must find wind wrapped in paper. Now go, and have a safe journey."*

The young women are overjoyed at the prospect of

seeing their family again, and they give no thought to the conditions. They pack their clothes and set out on foot. When they arrive at their village, they tell everyone of their new life, their husbands and their rich Father-in-law.

Then one day they realize that a fortnight has passed and that they cannot get back home on time. As they hurry along the road, they remember the gifts that they must take to their Father-in-law because a fortnight has passed.

"How can there be fire wrapped in paper?" wails the older sister.

"Where can I find wind wrapped in paper?" cries the younger girl.

Suddenly they hear a voice, though they see no one. *"Here is paper. Put a candle inside it."*

A paper lantern suddenly appears at their feet.

"Why, it's a lantern!" exclaims the older sister. *"Now I shall be forgiven for being late."*

"But what about me?" says her sister. *"I have nothing to take. What shall I do?"*

Again the voice speaks. *"Take this paper. See–it is folded so that you can fan yourself, bringing the wind to your face."*

No sooner are the words spoken than a fan appears on the ground. The young woman picks it up. *"It's a fan. Wind wrapped in paper!"*

When the two finally arrive home, they show the gifts to their Father-in-law. He is delighted with such marvelous inventions. In fact, they may have been the first lantern and the first fan in Japan.

THE TALKING CAT
(A French Canadian Folk Tale)

Characters

Tante Odette, an old woman
Chouchou, her cat
Pierre, a workman
Georges, his friend

There is an old woman, who is fooled into believing that her cat can speak. Tante Odette lives alone on her farm, deep in the Canadian woods. She is careful and thrifty, always keeping a pot of soup on the stove for herself and her old gray cat, Chouchou. She takes good care of her small farm. But as the years go by, she sometimes complains that the work is becoming too much for her. She talks to Chouchou about the chores that have to be done and how she must save her money for later. Often she says to him, *"How I wish you could talk, Chouchou. Then I should not be so lonely."*

One evening as Tante Odette is sitting by the fire, there is a knock at the door. When she opens it, she sees a man in workman's clothes with a red sash tied around his waist.

"I am looking for work," he says politely, *"If you can give me some chores, all I ask is a bowl of soup and a night's sleep in your barn."*

"Go away," says Tante Odette. *"I do not need anyone to help me. Besides, I have only enough soup for myself."*

Just as she is about to close the door in his face, an amazing thing happens. Chouchou speaks! *"Wait a minute,"* he says. *"You are getting older, and it would be a good idea to have a strong young man on the place."*

Tante Odette can't believe her ears. She looks at the man; then she looks at the cat. "*Well, if you think so, Chouchou.*"

"I certainly do," says the cat. *"Ask him to come in and join us in a bowl of soup."*

The old woman invites the man in and asks him to supper. *"It's only cabbage soup and bread, but we like it."*

The man thanks her. When he has finished his supper, he tells her tales of his travels and the different places he has worked. But he says that now he would rather stay in one place, even though he wouldn't make any money. He tells her his name is Pierre. As time goes on both the old woman and Chouchou become very fond of him.

One day Chouchou says to Tante Odette, *"Why don't you give Pierre meat and cakes? He works hard. I'm sure he gets very hungry."*

"But we have no meat," she replies.

"Then let him go to the store in the town and buy some meat. He will not waste your money."

Pierre appears in the doorway. *"I heard what your cat said just now. He's very wise. Let me strike a good bargain."*

The old woman goes to a chest of drawers and takes out some money. *"Mind you don't waste it,"* she tells Pierre.

When Pierre has gone, she turns to Chouchou. *"How is it that you never spoke in all the years that I've had you and now you are giving me advice?"*

But as always, when they are alone, Chouchou says nothing.

The next day when they finish their dinner of meat and cakes, Pierre is in a very good mood and Tante Odette says that she has never enjoyed a meal so much! *"Why don't you let Pierre move into the house?"* asks the cat.

"What?" says the old woman.

"Winter is coming and it will soon be cold in the barn. We have plenty of room inside."

Pierre says that he would like this very much. And so he moves in.

A few weeks later when the old woman is alone in the house, there is a knock at the door. She opens it and to her surprise, she sees a working man standing there. He is wearing a red sash just like Pierre's.

"Have you seen a workman who calls himself Pierre?" the newcomer asks.

"A man by that name works for me," the old woman says.

"Is he a good worker?"

"A very good worker," she says; and she tells of all the things Pierre can do.

"It certainly sounds like the same man. One more thing, can he throw his voice? Is he a ventriloquist?"

"Throw his voice? Oh, no! I could not stand having anyone around who did that."

"Then it can't be the same person," says the man, as he turns to go.

At this moment Pierre comes to the door. *"Georges!"* he shouts, *"My old friend!"*

"Pierre! I've been searching for you everywhere. I want you to go with me to get furs. You know they pay good money for furs in the city. How about it?"

Pierre thinks for a moment. *"If I go with you, I'll make money, but it will be cold. If I stay here, I have a good job, food, and a warm place to sleep. What shall I do, Chouchou? You're a wise cat."*

"Stay here," the cat answers. Then the cat turns to the old woman. *"Why don't we pay him some wages? You have money in the chest. Surely he's worth a few pieces of gold."*

The old woman doesn't know what to do. Finally she says, *"Very well. I can give you a small wage, if you'll stay."*

"Good!" said Pierre. *"Then I'll stay."* He says goodbye to his friend and walks with him down the road.

The old woman looks at Chouchou. *"I don't believe he throws his voice, do you?"*

There was no answer. She stares at Chouchou, who says nothing as usual.

Just then Pierre returns. *"It will be a much better winter for me here than in the north woods. And I can earn money at the same time, thanks to your cat."*

The cat bows and speaks.

"That's all right, Pierre. Fair is fair." Then Chouchou looks at the old woman. *"Well, we may as well sit down at the table and celebrate the way it has all worked out."*

GEORGE, THE TIMID GHOST

Characters

Father Ghost *George*

There is a timid ghost named George. He lives with his father and mother at the edge of a cemetery not far from a town. He wants very much to be able to scare people like a proper ghost, but every time someone approaches him, he runs away. *"Some day,"* he often says to himself, *"I'll be as spooky as the rest of my family. Some day, but not today."*

One night George's father decides it is time to teach his son a lesson. When it is quite dark, George's father shows him how to sneak up behind someone without being heard, and to say *"Boo!" "Never hurt anyone,"* his father warns him. *"Just give them a little scare."*

George is eager to learn all of his father's tricks, so he practices saying *"Boo"* in different tones of voice. He jumps out from behind trees, and he runs back and forth waving his arms in the air.

"Good," says his father approvingly. *"You're going to be the scariest ghost in town."*

George struts back and forth after his father goes into the house. *"I'm going to be the scariest ghost in town."*

Suddenly he hears the sound of somebody running. He freezes in his steps, determined not to run away.

This is an unfinished story. What happens next? You make up the ending.

CHAPTER SIX
Making Up Your Own Plays

It's fun to act out stories you know, but it's just as much fun to make up plays of your own. They may be about things that have really happened or things you imagine.

PLAYS ABOUT YOUR HOME AND YOUR NEIGHBORHOOD

The best way to start is with the people and places you know—*you,* your *family* and *friends,* your school, and the things you do. You might try this idea for a starter.

A MISTAKE

Characters

You
Your Family (They talk offstage.)

You come to breakfast early in the morning, but no one is there. You call your mother, but she tells you to be quiet. She is trying to sleep. You find some food to eat. Then you get your books and pack a lunch. You call to your family and tell them that they will all be late. You run out of the house, but a minute later you come back in. Your father calls to ask who it is. You tell him that the school bus isn't there. He laughs and says, "Of course, not. Did you forget? Daylight Saving Time is over!"

TROUBLE

Characters

You—a finger puppet
The Other Person—a glove puppet

Most of us get into trouble at various times. Remember a particular time when you got into trouble? Was it your fault? Do you think you were punished unfairly? How did you feel about it? Let your glove puppet be the other person in this story and act it out.

LOST IN THE WOODS

Character

You

Have you ever been lost? If you have, do you remember how you felt? Imagine that you're on a school picnic and have wandered away from the group. Suddenly you find yourself in a part of the woods you have never seen before. You call, but no one hears you. What happens? How do you find your way back?

LOST IN A DEPARTMENT STORE

Characters

You
A Clerk
The Store Manager
Your Mother

When you were little, did you ever get lost in a big store? Imagine that you are shopping with your mother in a department store at Christmas time. You are looking at bicycles, and you don't see her walking away. Suddenly you realize you are alone. You try to find her, but you are lost. You tell a Clerk, but she is too busy to help you. At last you see the Manager. How does he help you?

TALKING WITH YOUR PUPPET

Here is an idea that can be lots of fun. Like a conversation with a person, it will build as it goes along.

1. Imagine that your puppet is mischievous.

You ask it to do something and it refuses. It thinks of reasons why it won't do what you ask. How do you handle the puppet? Who wins?

2. Imagine that your puppet is angry, and that you try to find out what is wrong.
3. Imagine that your puppet can't speak English. Try to make it understand you.
4. Imagine that your puppet's feelings are hurt. Can you say or do anything to make it feel better?

THE PUPPET IS YOU

Imagine that the puppet is *you,* and talk to it as if you were one or any of the following: your mother, your best friend, the owner of a candy store in your neighborhood, your teacher, a new neighbor on the block.

YOU PLAY TWO PARTS

Put a big paper-bag puppet on your head and a small paper-bag puppet on your hand. Pretend the small puppet is you. The big puppet can be any one of the following: a giant, a mountain, a house, a school principal, the Loch Ness monster.

PUPPET PLAYS FOR SPECIAL DAYS

You may have to make some special puppets for this first play.

HALLOWEEN

Characters

Ghost
Witch
Goblin
Monster
Bat Scarecrow
Pumpkin

Have each character come out and tell how it can scare people. Try to make up a "spooky" story for each.

VALENTINE'S DAY

Characters

You
The Lady Next Door
Your Sister or Brother

It's Valentine's Day, and you didn't get any valentines. You feel very badly. You don't want to tell your brother or sister about it. Then the Lady Next Door enters. She says your mail was left in her box, and she gives you all the valentines you hoped you would get.

BIRTHDAYS

Characters

You
Your Family

Did you ever get a present that you didn't want? Or *not* get one that you wanted more than anything in the world? Make up a story about what happened and how you felt.

OTHER PLAYS

SPACE TRAVEL

There are all kinds of ideas about space travel that you can use for plays. Some things can be true. Or you can make up stories. For instance:

1. Imagine an astronaut landing on the moon or on Mars. How does he move? Make your puppet walk in space, and show what he finds and sees.
2. Imagine you are walking in the country, where you meet a man from another planet. His spaceship has landed in a field nearby. He wants to know who you are, where you live, what you do, and what you eat. Then he tells you about himself.

CIRCUS

You may need some special puppets, both animals and people. Try making flat ones, since they will be easier. You might like a clown, a ringmaster, a dancing bear, an acrobat, wild animals, or other characters.

MAGIC

What about a play with magic? Here are a few ideas for plays about magic. You'll no doubt think of many more.

Putting a spell on someone.
Finding a magic box and discovering what's in it.
Getting lost in a haunted house.

You can make up hundreds of plays. All you need is your imagination!